15 HOT MARKETS WHERE YOU CAN EASILY SELL YOUR BOOK ANYTIME

How to find profitable target markets and identify those who will gladly buy your books and become loyal customers of your author brand.

IREDAFENEVESHO OWOLABI

Some other Fast-selling Books By the author are:

- Kingdom Verities
- How to Enjoy Kingdom Currency (Vol. 1)
- How to Maximize Kingdom Currency (Vol. 2)
- Kingdom Currency for Students, Graduates and Businessmen (Vol. 3)
- Unlocking Your Kingdom Creativity
- 4-D THINKING
- Why you should Write a Book
- How to Turn your Knowledge to Money
- How to Turn Wisdom Currency to Money
- How to Make Millions as an Author-preneur
- 18 Steps to Write a Book Successfully
- How to Launch, Sell and Market your Books Profitably
- How to Successfully Self-Publish Your Books
- Hot Markets Where You Can Easily Sell Your Books
- CREATIVITY ACCELERATOR

All books are available for bulk purchase, please contact us via Tel: (+234) 8187960599.

 Or

Visit *www.iredafeowolabi.net/shop* for eBooks, Audiobooks, Video and Online programs by the author.

To Contact the author for feedbacks, to share or tell a story perhaps for inclusion in one of the future books by the author or to schedule him for a presentation, kindly send a mail to *info@iredafeowolabi.net* **or** *iredafeowolabi@gmail.com*.

TABLE OF CONTENT

MARKET ONE

THOSE WHO VALUE YOUR MESSAGE

There are people all over the world who are hungry for what you have to say. They want to hear your message and all you need do is to package it in form of information products and put them out so that those who know the value could buy them. You must understand that not everyone in your immediate circle would value your content and buy into it immediately. I have experienced the feeling of despair and disappointment that follows when people who you think should value your product turn out to be the ones who have no esteem whatsoever for them. It can be discouraging but you must know that there is a market for your book as long as it is designed to fix a real problem. All that you need to do is to locate those who know the value of your message, skill, knowledge, experience or expertise. Mind you, even your closest friends may not value your book so do not feel bad if they do not buy it. Just identify those who would appreciate and celebrate your work and you would find that there are more people willing to buy your books than you can even sell to.

MARKET TWO

THOSE WHO VALUE YOU

There are people who value your person, your story, your experience and impact. Probably they have heard about your exploits and hence have a good estimation of you. That could spur them to go get your books in order to learn more from your wealth of wisdom. That is why as an author you must be strategic and conscious as you go about your everyday life and interact with people. You must help them see your value and potential to add value to their lives. That way, you make it easy for them to believe they can gain from your books if they get them. And when that happens, they would not hesitate to buy from you.

MARKET THREE

THOSE WHO BELIEVE IN YOU

There are people who have seen the potentials and gifts that you are loaded with and that has caused them to believe in you and in your ability. They believe that you are an inspiration and hence want to get your books so that they can be part of your journey and enjoy from your content.

MARKET FOUR

THOSE WHO WANT TO LEARN FROM YOU

There are people who want to learn from you because they have seen you demonstrate superior skill and expertise in a particular area. These people may want to also replicate your kind of results in their own lives and this may cause them to search out your written works so that they can learn your secrets. They decide to become your students by getting your books, audio books, audio programs, and what have you, so that they could know what you know and much more. These are people who look up to you and are seeking ways to model or pattern their journey after yours. No matter who you are and what you are yet to achieve, as long as you are some steps ahead in anything worthy of admiration, applause or recognition, there are a bunch of people out there who seek you to be their role model or mentor. These people may not come to meet you to tell you personally but when they know you have published books on relevant topics, they would find it easy to connect with you and gain from your wisdom, stories, knowledge, skill or expertise. They believe you have mastered the trade or art they want to learn and practice and so they would consider your books as a great place to start.

MARKET FIVE

THOSE WHO KNOW YOUR BRAND

The moment people know your brand and what your brand projects, they would become loyal to you and would not hesitate to get your books once it is available. People who know my brand know that I always write great books so whenever they hear that there is a new book in the offing, they begin to salivate in anticipation. They wait for its release with excitement and as always, they never get disappointed because the value I deliver through my books always increases. You must work on projecting yourself as a good brand for people to buy your product. People call me "kingdom man" today because of the uniqueness of my message and that has formed a very integral part of my brand. You need a solid brand especially as a budding author who wants to make an impact. Do not scatter yourself around so many niches or topics at the same time when starting out. Focus on one topic that you know you command results or have experience with. Develop your brand around that idea until people can call your name as a synonym relating to that topic. For example, when people hear the name "John Maxwell", they already have an expectation because his name is synonymous with leadership. Even though he has some books on some other topical issues now, he has built a strong brand around leadership such that people would not mind buying from him when he writes on something slightly different from leadership.

MARKET SIX

THOSE WHO THINK YOU HAVE SOMETHING THEY NEED TO HEAR

A lot of aspiring authors erroneously think that one needs to become an expert at writing before he can write a book that would be worth reading. They could not be further from the truth because the so-called experts were once novices. The only way to become an expert at writing is to write, write and write! There are no short cuts to it at all. All you need is to be sure you have something that people think they need to hear. It has to be a unique angle to something they know or do not know. It could also be something slightly similar and related to what they have known before or a fresh perspective to something they want to hear about. There are ways you can know people who may fall into this category. People who admire your skill and prowess or who may need some advice in an area where you seem to have gained mastery would gladly buy your books to help themselves get more insights into your knowledge.

MARKET SEVEN

THOSE WHOSE PROBLEMS YOUR CONTENT SOLVES

When people know that your content was tailored in a manner that is inclusive of them, they would buy your books. People whose problems and needs your book was designed for would buy your book. It is one thing to say my book is for youths but it is another thing entirely for these youths to see your book as an item they can consult to get a particular problem or an array of problems solved. If your book is designed with people's problems in mind and it goes ahead to solve these problems, it would not be difficult to get buyers for them with the right strategies in place.

MARKET EIGHT

THOSE WHO HAVE HEARD OTHER PEOPLE'S FEEDBACK

No matter how great your product is there are people who would not give it a try until they hear that Mr. ABC has used that product and had a good experience. The same thing goes for a book. There are lots of people who can be classified as late buyers and these people only buy a book when they hear the way people are testifying about it. That is why it is too important to have a system that can allow readers of your work to make comments about their experience when they read your book. Most times, greater sales are generated from referrals compared to sales got from direct marketing or direct advertisements. So, the moment your how-to book is proved to be something that works, there are a bunch of others who would automatically want to buy it for what it is worth.

MARKET NINE

THOSE WHO WANT TO ENCOURAGE

YOU

This accounts for a few of your acquaintances who believe in your message and really want to do more than just buy your book so they give you grants and good launch packages. They also give you opportunities within their capacity that would help you get more books into the hands of people who may want to get them. They are people who love your drive and your passion because of the commitment and dedication they see you putting into what you are doing. This category of people is rare to find. These are also the group of people who would give you generous grants without being asked just because they want to encourage you to keep making an impact. These are people who would launch your book in a rather lavish manner. They do this not because they do not have any better use for their money but because they see a bright future ahead of you and want to be a part of your success story. You may not always have these people around you in the beginning of your journey. You must therefore remain determined to make a difference nonetheless, whether you get a pat on your back or not. In my own time as a budding author, I had a number of people who were drawn toward me and went out of their way to support my work in many different ways. People like my wonderful mother, my amazing father, my loving wife and my big sister have been exceptional in their own unique way. I have also witnessed lots of encouragement from family friends, acquaintances and from people I didn't really know or expect anything from. Each and every one of these people was God's way of helping me achieve most of the results I have realized today. I am making this known to you because most times, you see celebrity writers and famous author-preneurs who never tell their story. They make it sound like they made it all the way to the top on their own. For me, I had encouragers, and I want you to also know that there are people on your pathway that God has ordained to help you fulfil your potential through it all. You may never see them until you begin to take the bold step and begin to disrupt with your novelty. Trust me I also get my own fair share of discouragements. It has not been all rosy but I cannot deny the role the little encouragements I get here and there have played for me as an author-preneur.

MARKET TEN

THOSE WHO HAVE HEARD YOU SPEAK AND WERE INSPIRED

One of the easiest sales you would ever make is going to be sales made to people who listened to your keynote speech, presentation, attended your seminar or partook in a training you facilitated. If you speak to these people and you are able to get them fired up, they would be the ones looking for what more they can get from your vast store of wisdom or knowledge. The moment they find out that you have books, they would eagerly want to get them in a bid to learn more from you. Never be shy to make it known to your audience that you have a book that may be of benefit to them as a speaker, except you do not believe they can benefit from what you have written.

MARKET ELEVEN

THOSE WHO LOVE READING ON THE SUBJECT MATTER YOU WROTE ABOUT

Many different people have topics that interest them. There are people who are obsessed with reading books that are comic related, money related, romance related, health related, job related, business related or industry related. They have developed so much love, passion and curiosity for these topical issues that when they see a book that appears to address their concerns, they go for it regardless of how famous or not-so-famous the author is. That is why you should make sure you are writing about something that is so compelling and could command a great deal of interest for readers. That is the easiest way to get seen, heard and paid.

MARKET TWELVE

THOSE WHO NEED IT TO ACHIEVE

RESULTS

As long as your book is tailored to help people achieve an objective or get a desired result, it would make a good read for such folks. It is best that you also have some testimonials, proofs, personal experiences or results to show as you write so that people would be better persuaded that your book can help them get the results they are looking for.

MARKET THIRTEEN

THOSE WHO BELIEVE IT WILL HELP THEM SOLVE A PROBLEM

If your book is a solution bank, people who need to eradicate a problem would be more than willing to get it. There are myriad problems in the world today and people are in a constant search for some knowledge, secret or discovery that would help them overcome the various challenges that stares them in the face.

MARKET FOURTEEN

THOSE WHO WERE ATTRACTED TO THE TITLE AND COVER DESIGN

Not many have yet heeded to the counsel that says "do not judge a book by its cover". Most people in the larger majority of the book market make their buying decisions based on the book title and book cover. If you are not yet a famous author, then you must not take for granted the kind of title you give your book or the design that goes with it. That would go a long way to attract paying customers to your book.

MARKET FIFTEEN

THOSE WHO WANT TO HEAR YOUR STORY

People who would be interested in hearing your story form one of your greatest tribe. If you have come through some difficulty in life and seem to be making your way through, you have what it takes to wow your readers. Just know that there would always be someone out there who would love to hear the stories behind your experiences of success or failure. That story of yours could become a glimmer of hope for those coming behind you who may be facing a similar difficulty. Maybe your story is even a fictitious one that has a great twist and tale to it. There are millions of people out there who would find it appealing. The market for stories and story books including fictional tales is growing so fast and as long as you get your book development and sales processes right, you would get people to buy them.

ABOUT THE AUTHOR

Iredafenevesho Owolabi (Iredafe or Dafe for short) is a Creativity Coach with the goal of helping individuals and organizations move from idea to profitable creations. He redefines public speaking with cutting-edge kingdom insights. He is happily married to the love of his life.

His books are being read in different parts of the world with countless testimonials of their impact. He mentors several aspiring authors to success via coaching calls and his book titled "How to Make Millions as An Author-preneur" is a must-have for all authors and aspiring author-preneurs who intend to master the business of their writing gift.

He speaks to different professionals and seminars via his seminars focusing on topics like Authorpreneurship, Creativity, 4-D Thinking, Unlocking Potential, Reinvention, Kingdom etc. To invite him or schedule him for a presentation, send him a mail via iredafeowolabi@gmail.com.

For tips and information on how to publish and market your books successfully and effectively, get

"How to Make Millions as An Authorpreneur" and other books by Iredafenevesho Owolabi.

His Books include:

- Kingdom Verities
- How to Enjoy Kingdom Currency (Vol. 1)
- How to Maximize Kingdom Currency (Vol. 2)
- Kingdom Currency for Students, Graduates and Businessmen (Vol. 3)

- Kingdom Money
- Unlocking Your Kingdom Creativity
- 4-D THINKING
- Why you should Write a Book
- How to Turn your Knowledge to Money
- How to Turn Wisdom Currency to Money'
- How to Make Millions as an Author-preneur
- 18 Steps to Writing a Book Successfully
- How to Launch, Sell and Market your Books Profitably
- How To Self-Publish Your Books

And lots more.

They are all available on Amazon in different formats.

www.ingramcontent.com/pod-product-compliance
Lightning Source LLC
Chambersburg PA
CBHW030552220526
45463CB00007B/3068